Travel Guide and Journal for Kids

Going to Toronto

T. Attard

B. Grabowski

tellwell

Going to Toronto

tellwell

Tellwell Talent
www.tellwell.ca

ISBN
978-1-988186-93-1 (Paperback)

This book is dedicated to the parents and
those who believe that travel opens up new
doors and experiences, and to the children,
lucky enough to go through those doors.

Table of Contents

Name:

Age:

Grade and School:

City you live in:

Country you live in:

Date of your vacation:

Welcome to Toronto

Reflection of Toronto

Reflection of Toronto

Hi there,

We just heard that you and your parents are planning a trip to Toronto, Canada. Well, you are in for a fun time. Toronto is a great city to visit, and there is lots to do. Maybe you live in Toronto and your parents have decided to explore your own city this year. Or, possibly you are visiting from another part of the province or country. For those of you who are coming from another country, let us say, "Welcome to Canada." Hope you enjoy yourself in this wonderful country and city.

Toronto is the largest city in Canada. It is in the province of Ontario and is situated on Lake Ontario, one of the 5 Great Lakes. It is also the capital of Ontario.

Once you are in the city, you will begin to understand why we are considered a Mosaic. A subway ride will give you the opportunity to experience the world in one city. Toronto is made up of many different communities living here. Each community brings its own culture and traditions. You can eat your way around the world in Toronto.

You have museums, galleries, islands, zoos, parks, Forts, amusement parks, sports and a wealth of other things to do in Toronto. When you are here, you many be lucky enough to participate in one or more of the many events that take place during the year, such as: Santa Claus Parade, The Exhibition, Royal Winter Fair, Pride Day, Taste of the Danforth, or the Toronto Caribbean Carnival, just to mention a few.

We hope that you enjoy this great city, and get to participate in many different activities. Have lots of fun and take lots of pictures.

Your friends,

Barbara and Therese

On Your Way!

1. Your full name as in your passport: ______________________

2. Date of trip: ______________________

3. Where are you travelling to? ______________________

4. Who is travelling with you? ______________________

____

5. What city or town are you leaving from? ______________________

6. What airport or train station are you leaving from or are you travelling by car? ______________________

7. Time you left home: ______________________

8. Time you arrived at airport or train station: ______________________

9. Time of flight or train departure: ______________________

10. Name of airline or rail-line you are travelling with: ______________

11. Your flight or train number: ______________________

12. Your gate or platform number: ______________________

13. Your seat number: ______________________

14. Did you go through a security check? ______________________

15. What did you do during the flight or train ride? ______________
____
____

16. What did you eat during the trip? ______________________
____
____

17. What country did you arrive in ? ______________________

18. What city did you arrive in? ______________________

19. What is the name of the airport or train station? ______________

20. What time did you arrive? ______________________

21. Did you enjoy your flight or train ride to your destination?

Likes	Dislikes
____________________	____________________
____________________	____________________
____________________	____________________
____________________	____________________

22. Did you go through customs? ____________________

23. Did they stamp your passport? ____________________

24. Are you staying with family or friends tonight? ____________

25. Did your parents rent an apartment? ____________________

OR

26. Are you staying in a hotel? ____________________

27. If so, what is the name of the hotel? ____________________

28. Did you get on another plane, train or into a car to get to Toronto?

____

29. What time did you unpack your suitcase? ______________

30. What is the date? ____________________

31. How many hours have you been travelling? ______________

Houses in Winter

Your Vacation is Just Beginning -- Have Fun!

Describe where you are staying. ______________________________

How is this place different from your place at home? Try and list 10 things that are the same and 10 things that are different. If you can't, list as many as possible.

Things that are the same

Things that are different

Things I Don't Want to Forget

On Your Way

Unscramble the letters — not too difficult!

1. I T R P
2. X A I T
3. U N F
4. T F G L I H
5. C T I E S S A U
6. I N A R T
7. N E P I L R A A
8. U R L A N J O
9. K A P C
10. O O T T O N R
11. O E H T L
12. R I O T O A N
13. D A A A N C
14. E A T G
15. F L M O R A P T

Canada

Canada is the 2nd largest country in the world by area - after Russia - and the largest in the continent of North America. Its population is about 36 million people. The 2 official languages are English and French. Canada is made up of 10 provinces and 3 territories. Each province has its own

capital, government and Premier. The capital of Canada is Ottawa, in the province of Ontario, where you will also find our Federal Parliament led by the Prime Minister of Canada.

Canada is surrounded by 3 oceans: Pacific Ocean to the west, Arctic Ocean to the north and Atlantic Ocean to the east. Our southern border - the International Boundary - makes us neighbours with the United States of America and the State of Alaska to the northwest. The Canada - US border is 6,422 km (3,989 mi) in length and crosses 6 time zones covering 4 1/2 hours.

Canada - meaning village - is known for its varied and open landscape. Sky-high mountains which makeup the Rockies are found in British Columbia and Alberta. Glaciers, whales and polar bears can be found in the Arctic Ocean and Hudson Bay. There are many rivers and lakes throughout the country. Plains and farmlands are found in Saskatchewan, Alberta, Manitoba and Quebec. Our Maritime provinces are known for their fisheries.

Canada shares 4 of the 5 Great Lakes with the United States. Lake Michigan is the only one that lies entirely within the United States. An easy way to remember their names is to think of H.O.M.E.S.- Huron, Ontario, Michigan, Erie and Superior. The Great Lakes makeup the largest body of fresh water in the world - about 20%. These lakes are still used as a gateway to the Atlantic Ocean by way of the St. Lawrence River.

Canada continues to be known as a multicultural country that respects its various cultures, traditions and First Nations. It is a massive country that varies in its people, landscape, climate and way of life.

Provincial Flag Map of Canada

Provinces & Territories of Canada & Their Capitals

PROVINCE	PROVINCIAL CAPITALS
1. British Columbia	1. Victoria
2. Alberta	2. Edmonton
3. Saskatchewan	3. Regina
4. Manitoba	4. Winnipeg
5. Ontario	5. Toronto
6. Quebec	6. Quebec City
7. New Brunswick	7. Fredericton
8. Nova Scotia	8. Halifax
9. Prince Edward Island	9. Charlottetown
10. Newfoundland	10. St. John's
11. Yukon Territory	11. Whitehorse
12. Northwest Territory	12. Yellowknife
13. Nunavut	13. Iqaluit

Flags of Country - Province - City

Canadian Flag

The Canadian Flag is known as the Maple Leaf. It made its first appearance on February 15, 1965. Prime Minister Lester B. Pearson was determined for Canada to have its own flag before the celebration of Canada's 100th birthday, July 1, 1967. The Maple Leaf has been used as a Canadian symbol since the 1700's.

During World War I, Lester Pearson noted that most of the Canadian soldiers wore the Maple Leaf proudly as part of their battalion crest. He never forgot that, and promised upon being elected Prime Minister, that Canada would fly its own flag, and that flag would include the Maple Leaf.

On October 22, 1964, the Maple Leaf Flag was passed in Parliament. The debate which lasted 33 days between Prime Minister Pearson and the Leader of the Opposition, John Diefenbaker, a former Prime Minister, was finally voted in.

Even though Canada was independent of Britain since July 1, 1867, it took 97 years before a flag was raised without some form of the British Union Jack.

The colours, red and white were proclaimed by King George as the official colours of Canada in 1921. The red came from the St. George's Cross and the white from the French Royal Emblem, recognizing the bi-lingual and bi-cultural identity of Canada. The French nickname for the Canadian Flag is "L' Unfoldie," meaning one-leafed.

The Maple Leaf is a very recognizable flag with its brilliant red, 11 pointed maple leaf on a snow white background.

Ontario Flag

The Ontario Flag was first seen on May 21, 1965. In the upper corner, called the Canton, is the Union Jack of the United Kingdom. In the opposite corner, called the Fly, is the Ontario Shield of Ams. The main colour of the flag is red. The Ontario Shield of Arms consists of 3 golden maple leaves on a green background below the St. George Cross. The Ontario Shield of Arms was granted to Ontario by Queen Victoria in 1868.

Toronto Flag

The Toronto Flag was designed by Rene de Santis, a 21 year old George Brown College student. He won the competition in 1974 with his design, using the colours red, white and blue. Two white towers representing the towers of the City Hall are placed on a blue background. At the base is the red Maple Leaf, representing Canada. The white towers form the letter T for Toronto.

Ontario

Ontario is one of the four original provinces which formed Canada in 1867. The other three are Quebec, New Brunswick, and Nova Scotia. Before Confederation in1867, Ontario was called Upper Canada.

The province is bordered by the province of Quebec on the east and Manitoba on the west. The southern border of the province follows the Great Lakes and the St. Lawrence River. In the north, the shoreline follows James Bay and Hudson Bay.

Ontario is a land of lakes and rivers. About 1/5th of the world's fresh water can be found in Ontario. A visit to Niagara Falls is very easy from Toronto, or you can go in the opposite direction and spend a day in the Thousand Islands. Travel north of Toronto and you will find wonderful lakes and small towns to visit.

The population of Ontario is approximately 14 million. More than 2/3rd live in the southern part of the province, called the Golden Horseshoe. The Horseshoe is a strip of land which follows the western end of Lake Ontario, in the shape of a horseshoe.

The capital of Ontario is Toronto. Ottawa, the capital of Canada, is also in Ontario. It is situated on the Ottawa River which forms a natural boundary with the province of Quebec.

The name Ontario comes from an Iroquois word meaning **"Beautiful Lake or Beautiful Water"** which describes the province.

Enjoy your time in Ontario. There is lots to do all year round. Hopefully, this will be one of your many visits to the province.

Map of Ontario

Toronto

Toronto - Canada's largest city - is located on the northwest shore of Lake Ontario in the province of Ontario. With a population of 2.8 million people, it is said to be one of the most multicultural cities in the world. It has also been ranked as the safest large metropolitan area in North America. The name of the city comes from the Huron word **"Tkaronto"** which stands for fishing weir, a structure that is put into water to trap fish!

The city of Toronto is about 388 sq. km. (243 miles) and sits on top of sedimentary rock. It stretches 43 km. (25 miles) from east to west and 21 km. (12 miles) from north to south. Three major rivers run through the city - Humber River in the west, Don River in the middle and the Rouge River in the east. All flow into Lake Ontario.

Toronto is often described as a mosaic where many different cultures live and play together. Officially, there are 140 neighbourhoods, each with their own identities, food, traditions, customs and music. As you walk around Toronto and visit the different neighbourhoods, notice the street signs and store front names that are often written in their own language.

Toronto is home to many professional teams such as Toronto Argonauts (football), Toronto Blue Jays (baseball), Toronto FC (soccer), Toronto Maple Leafs (hockey), Toronto Marlies (junior hockey), Toronto Raptors (basketball) and Toronto Rock (lacrosse). You can watch these teams play at the Air Canada Centre (ACC), Rogers Centre or BMO field.

As an education-focused city, Toronto is home to 8 publicly funded post-secondary schools - 4 universities that include University of Toronto, York University, Ryerson University and Ontario College of Art and Design University and 4 colleges - Humber College, George Brown College, Seneca College and Centennial College.

Over 40 hospitals are located in Toronto. Many are also medical research facilities and teaching schools. Hospital for Sick Children continues to be a leader in children research, education and care. Toronto General Hospital is ranked as the best research hospital in Canada. Princess Margaret Hospital continues to lead in the treatment of cancer.

Enjoy this amazing city. Get on the Red Rocket - our red streetcars - and begin exploring our museums, art galleries, castles, different foods and various festivals throughout the year!

True or False

1. Toronto is on Lake Ontario. T or F
2. Toronto is the capital of Ontario. T or F
3. Canada is bordered by 3 Oceans. T or F
4. The capital of Canada is Ottawa. T or F
5. There are 7 Great Lakes. T or F
6. The longest street in the world is in Toronto. T or F
7. Canada's southern neighbour is the U.S.A. T or F
8. There are 6 Time Zones in Canada. T or F
9. The Oak Leaf is the symbol on the Canadian Flag. T or F
10. The Blue Jays are Toronto's hockey team. T or F
11. Ontario is one of the original provinces of Canada. T or F
12. Canada is the largest country in the world. T or F
13. Canada became a country on July 1, 1867. T or F
14. There are 10 Provinces and 3 Territories in Canada. T or F
15. The Maple Leaf became Canada's Flag on February 15, 1965. T or F

What do I know about Toronto?

1. Toronto's population is ______________________.
2. Lake ____________ borders Toronto.
3. ____________ and ____________ are provincial neighbours of Ontario.
4. ____________, ____________ and ____________ are 3 rivers that run through Toronto.
5. Toronto's baseball team is called ______________________.
6. The Raptors is Toronto's ____________ team.
7. There are ____________ different neighbourhoods in Toronto.
8. Our streetcars are called the ______________________.
9. What Toronto landmark can be seen from New York State on a clear day? ______________________
10. There are ____________ Great Lakes.
11. H.O.M.E.S stands for ____________, ____________, ____________, ____________ and ____________.
12. What was given as a gift to Toronto by Mr. and Mrs. Howard?

____

C.N. Tower

C.N. Tower by Lake Ontario

C.N. Tower

View through Glass Floor of Tower

The CN tower is Toronto's most recognizable symbol. It stands 553 m. (1815 feet) high and can be seen from 40 km. (25 miles) to the north, 60 km. (36 miles) to the east and 48 km. (29 miles) to the south in New York State.

In 1972, Canadian National (CN) set out to build a tower that would solve communication problems for both Toronto's citizens and various radio

stations. Work began on February 6, 1973 with 1,537 people working around the clock for 40 months - and was open to the public June 26, 1976. The cost was $63 million.

CN Tower is home to 3 public observation points. You can zip up in a glass-front elevator in just 58 seconds to get a great clear view of the city. Sky pod stands 447 m. (1467 feet) high, Indoor Observation Level is at 346 m. (1135 feet) and the Outdoor Observation Terrace has its heart-stopping Glass Floor at 342 m. (1122 feet). Don't worry - this floor is built to hold 35 moose!!

One floor above is the Top of Toronto restaurant which completes a revolution once every 90 minutes. Edgewalk - CN Tower's most thrilling attraction - elevation 356 m. (1168 feet) - allows visitors to be attached to an overhead safety rail while walking hands-free on a 1.5 m. (5 feet) wide ledge that circles the top of the Tower's main pod. Please remember - you must be 13 years old in order to participate.

In the evening, make sure that you look up to see the C.N. Tower light its 1,330 LED fixtures in red and white. A spectacular light show can be seen at the top of each hour at night every day.

Ripley's Aquarium

Ripley's Aquarium of Canada is this country's largest indoor aquarium showing more than 16,000 marine animals. Located next to the CN Tower, it is open every day and features one of the world's most extensive jelly fish exhibits, 65+ year old giant lobsters, stingrays and bamboo shark touch pools and daily live shows.

The aquarium has 5.7 million litres (1.5 million gallons) of marine and freshwater habitats. It is organized into 9 galleries: Canadian Waters, Rainbow Reef, Dangerous Lagoon, Discovery Centre, The Gallery, Ray Bay, Planet Jellies, Life Support Systems and the Shoreline Gallery.

Canadian Waters features animals from all bodies of water surrounding Canada such as American lobster, wolf eel, lump fish, giant Pacific octopus and China rock fish.

Rainbow Reef features animals from the Indo-Pacific water region and is the most colourful gallery in the aquarium. It also has an interactive dive show.

The Dangerous Lagoon is an underwater tunnel with a moving sidewalk that takes you through sharks, green sea turtles, sawfish, eels and Pacific sea nettle jelly fish that light up in different colours.

The Discovery Centre features different hands-on activities such as underwater viewing bubbles, pop-up research submarine and a touch pool allowing you to touch living fossils like sharks and stingrays.

The Gallery features some of the most delicate underwater species from all over the world such as the red lion fish, electric eel, lined seahorse and weedy sea dragon.

The Life Support System gives you a behind-the-scenes look at how the aquarium and its equipment work together.

Ripley's Aquarium has over 100 interactive and educational opportunities that include dive shows, feedings and hands-on touch exhibits. You and your family will experience unforgettable adventures.

Have fun today!

Jelly fish at Ripley's Aquarium

Fort York

Back entry into Fort York

Drill practice at Fort York

Fort York, located on the west side of downtown Toronto, is a historic museum site with various exhibits and restored period buildings. It is also the oldest structure in Toronto dating back to 1793.

The founding of urban Toronto was a military event that happened when John Graves Simcoe ordered the building of a Garrison in order to protect Lake Ontario from the United States. As Lieutenant-Governor of the British province of Upper Canada (Ontario), Simcoe moved the provincial capital from Niagara to Toronto - renaming it York. Relations between York (Toronto) and the U.S.A. began to weaken. In 1812, the United States declared war and invaded Canada. Overpowered by the strong American force, the British commander blew up the gunpowder magazine killing many soldiers on both sides. The Americans continued to occupy York for 6 days - looting, burning and destroying buildings and supplies. In 1814, the British responded by capturing the city of Washington and burning the White House and other buildings. Once again, the Americans returned to York to burn buildings and barracks they missed from before. Shortly after this, Fort York was rebuilt (today's site). In August 1814, the Americans were stopped from entering York by way of Lake Ontario. By February 1815, word came that the War of 1812 was over. Peace had returned. Canada no longer had to worry about an American invasion.

In years to come, Fort York was used for training of soldiers and as barracks, offices and storage. By 1934, it was opened as a historic site museum.

Today, the walls surround Canada's largest collection of original 1812 buildings. They also surround part of the 1813 battlefield and 2 cemeteries. Current buildings to visit and explore include the Stone Powder Magazine, North and South Soldier Barracks, Blockhouses 1 and 2, Officers Quarters, Blue Barracks, Brick Powder Magazine and the Lieutenant Governor's residence.

Don't miss the Fort York Armoury - located southwest - a 2 storey structure built in 1933. It's occupied by 3 active units of the Canadian Army Reserve - the Canadian Forces Primary Reserve, the Queen's York Rangers, the Royal Regiment of Canada and the 32 Signals Regiment and several thriving cadet organizations.

Queen's Quay boardwalk at Harbourfront

Nice way to end the day

Harbourfront

Harbourfront is a neighbourhood on the northern shore of Lake Ontario and within the downtown core of Toronto. This area was originally used for shipping and industrial purposes. In 1972, Prime Minister P. E. Trudeau announced a project to change this land into a cultural and residential area for the city. Today, this area is home to art galleries, a skating rink, performance spaces, boating areas and parks. To the north of Queen's Quay (pronounced "key") are high-rise condominium towers, to the east a hotel and ferry docks that will get you to Toronto Islands and Redpath Sugar Factory Museum.

During the summer, check out free concerts at Harbourfront's outdoor concert stage, visit Queen's Quay Terminal - a former warehouse changed into a shopping area with stores and restaurants. Visit the Redpath Sugar Refinery at the foot of Jarvis Street (east of the ferry docks) and explore the refinery and sugar production museum. Across the street is Sugar Beach, a sandy beach with lighting, umbrellas and muskoka chairs, a rocky amphitheatre and candy trim pedestrian areas paved in 3 colours that are arranged in the shape of a maple leaf.

Toronto Music Garden - located west near Spadina Rd- consists of beautiful gardens inspired by the music of J. S. Bach, great views of Lake Ontario, summer concerts, eco-programs and space to sit quietly and think about nature.

There is something to see and do for every member of your family everyday of the week. Have fun!!

Ferry returning from Centre Island

Views of Toronto from the Island

Toronto Islands

The Toronto Islands are a chain of small islands in the western part of Lake Ontario and just off the shore from the city centre. Formerly, the islands were called "Island of Hiawatha" and were also called " Menecing", a word meaning "on the island" in the First Nations Ojibwa language. The islands are home to parkland, a small residential community, several boat clubs, an amusement park, several sand beaches and Billy Bishop City Airport. Access to the islands is by ferry boat or water taxis, located at the foot of Bay St.

The islands form a crescent shape with Centre Island being the largest. To the east is Ward's Island and Algonquin Island, which have about 300 homes. To the west is Muggs Island and Toronto City Airport.

Centre Island is home to Centreville, a children's amusement park (ages 3 to 8) with a 1900's style theme. This park includes a miniature railway, an antique carousel, a swan ride and a mini roller coaster. Far Enough Farm is home to farm animals, livestock and birds. Franklin's Garden is a new children's garden located towards the western side. A splash pad and playground are nearby as is a flying disc golf course. Make sure you visit the Gibraltor Lighthouse which dates to 1808.

Several swimming beaches can be found at Centre Island Beach, Manitou Beach, Gibraltor Beach and Ward's Island Beach. Public tennis courts can be found at Hanlan's Point.

Olympic Island - east of the ferry terminal- offers the best view of downtown Toronto. It's large grassy field is perfect for picnics, BBQ's and picture taking.

Ward's Island and Algonquin Island are home to many of the Islands' residents. Although quieter and less busy, you can find the Queen City Yacht Club, the Rectory Cafe, the island fire station and the disc golf course. The boardwalk on the south side offers another great view of Lake Ontario.

Make sure you don't miss this little slice of heaven in Toronto.

Scrambled Words

1. HFSI ______________________________
2. QAUMRIAU ______________________________
3. EORWT ______________________________
4. PMLAE-AFLE ______________________________
5. SSDAINL ______________________________
6. LOERRL-AOCTSRE ______________________________
7. BECAH ______________________________
8. RRYFE-ATBO ______________________________
9. OTFR-KYRO ______________________________
10. LESDORI ______________________________
11. BCRAARSK ______________________________
12. ROFRARNOUBTH ______________________________
13. NEETCR-NDAISL ______________________________
14. UQYA ______________________________
15. EONYG-TTESRE ______________________________

Word Search

U	G	H	B	P	Z	X	C	F	C	A	T	H	E	D	R	A	L	Z
W	H	H	P	V	O	D	D	A	I	A	T	Y	X	K	T	X	I	P
K	Y	T	Y	M	Z	N	Q	G	S	W	F	O	J	C	Y	B	P	L
T	M	M	O	W	X	S	T	O	S	F	D	I	R	X	Z	S	M	Q
R	O	R	D	V	V	N	H	A	L	Y	O	N	H	O	A	O	O	A
G	K	K	I	A	X	A	H	J	R	D	T	R	U	A	N	E	B	T
C	C	S	S	P	C	J	E	A	R	I	G	H	T	A	V	T	T	T
K	L	S	T	H	L	N	Q	D	L	E	O	H	N	Y	B	E	O	R
S	O	J	I	N	E	E	T	T	J	L	D	O	C	P	O	M	F	M
T	A	O	L	R	F	O	Y	O	X	F	T	R	S	B	F	R	R	H
R	G	X	L	N	X	G	D	S	W	G	C	H	O	T	B	X	K	O
E	U	C	E	Q	Y	X	O	G	N	E	V	K	T	C	R	H	R	C
E	O	S	R	Q	Q	A	I	I	J	H	R	E	E	J	K	U	M	K
T	U	W	Y	C	D	F	S	E	H	S	K	M	Y	N	Q	E	G	E
C	R	P	T	A	I	N	Q	I	G	R	B	F	Y	Z	S	J	T	Y
A	U	F	N	B	E	C	Q	A	A	F	D	T	I	A	Q	R	B	X
R	U	A	E	K	O	I	W	M	J	G	J	E	K	R	N	M	J	P
X	C	Y	Q	J	G	P	N	F	K	M	V	F	T	I	L	K	M	C

* TORONTO
* DISTILLERY
* CATHEDRAL
* AGO
* FORT YORK
* HOCKEY
* ONTARIO
* CN TOWER
* CANADA
* ROM
* MARKET
* RIPLEYS
* STREETCAR
* KENSINGTON
* RED ROCKET

A page for you to either sketch something you saw that you want to remember. Or, record something you don't want to forget.

Toronto City Hall

Toronto flags at City Hall

Toronto City Hall

Toronto City Hall or New City Hall is home to the municipal (city) government of Toronto, Ontario. Designed by Finnish architect Viljo Revell, it is Toronto's most unique landmark. It opened in 1965 and was built to replace Old City Hall, which was built in 1899.

New City Hall consists of 2 unequal towers surrounding a white disk-like council chamber which is mounted on a raised platform with entrances below. A ramp connects the square to the podium roof. This building was nicknamed "the eye of the government."

The public square in front of city hall is named Nathan Phillips Square in honour of Toronto's mayor from 1955 to 1962. It is the site of concerts, public gatherings, art displays, a weekly farmer's market and our winter Festival of Lights. The Archer, by sculptor Henry Moore, is in front of the entrance. You can find another one of his works, in bronze, in front of the Art Gallery of Toronto (A.G.O.).

During the winter, the reflecting pool is turned into a skating rink. Spanning the pool are 3 concrete arches, supporting the rink lighting but also to commemorate those who fought to obtain and defend our freedom. A piece of the Berlin Wall was placed at the southern base of the arch, in 1989.

The Peace Garden- located on the western edge of the square - was created as a memorial to the atomic bombing of Hiroshima, Japan (August, 1945) and to all Torontonians for their wish for peace. A sundial is located at the south end of the garden. The garden consists of a pavilion, a fountain, surrounding plants and a stone-clad gazebo. One corner of this structure is damaged to represent conflict and the fragility of mankind. The eternal flame symbolizes Hope and was lit with an ember from the Peace Flame in Hiroshima by Pope John Paul II in September, 1984.

The square's new and permanent addition is the large, illuminated TORONTO sign, installed for the 2015 PanAm Games. Its popularity continues to grow. Don't forget to have your picture taken there!!

Skating at City Hall in winter.

Old City Hall

Old City Hall

Gargoyles of Old City Hall

Old City Hall

Old City Hall was Toronto's largest building and, at that time, the largest civic structure in North America. It was home to Toronto's city government from 1899 until 1966, when the New City Hall was open.

The building took 10 years to complete and cost over $25 million. Stonework was taken from local areas - sandstone from the Credit River, grey stone from Orangeville and brownstone from New Brunswick. At the front steps is the Cenotaph, erected in 1925 to honour Torontonians who died in World War I, World War II and the Korean War and peacekeeping missions. Four gargoyles were placed on the corners of the Clock Tower. Look for craved faces of the 1890 city councillors among the stonework of the triple-arch entrance, including the face of its architect - E. J. Lennox. He is the one with the handlebar moustache.

The interior of this building has a beautiful mosaic floor, detailed work tables, handrails and doorknobs that have the city's old coat of arms. Painted murals on the first floor by George A. Reid and the stained glass window, symbolizing Commerce and Industry, are works of art.

Today this building is used solely as a provincial courthouse. Its future is uncertain at this time.

Osgoode Hall

Osgoode Hall

Osgoode Hall

Osgoode Hall - a grand building occupying an entire city block - is named in honour of Ontario's first Chief Justice, William Osgoode. It is located to the west of New City Hall and is home to the highest courts of the province and the Law Society of Upper Canada (Ontario).

The building has gone through several expansions in order to accommodate courts, the law school and libraries. As of 1969, the law school moved to York University. The fence surrounding the lawns of Osgoode are unique, narrow and restrictive. An old myth suggests that the fences were designed to keep livestock out of the grounds. Check out the turning gate on the south side to see if this true.

The main doors open into the Rotunda or Atrium, a space noted for its geometric tiled floor and beautiful skylights. Ten courtrooms - some restored to their original beauty - give a feeling of seriousness throughout the halls.

Two libraries are housed inside Osgoode Hall - the Great Library of the Law Society of Upper Canada and a smaller library for the judges. The Great library has a detailed plaster ceiling and is home to the largest private collection of legal material in Canada.

The Benchers Wing - is the oldest section and has kept much of the Victorian style and character - mosaic floor, staircase, panelling and glass dome.

Convocation Hall was built as an examination room for law students. The stain glass windows were completed in 1989.

Osgoode Hall is adorned with portraits of past provincial Chief Justices and Treasurers of the Law Society.

As you walk through these halls and rooms, visitors feel the importance of following the laws of our country.

Gates of Osgoode Hall

Canadian Money

Canadian coin currency
$0.05, $0.10, $0.25, $0.50, $1.00, $2.00

The Penny or $0.01 disappeared on Feb. 4, 2013. It was removed because it cost more to make than what it was worth.

The $1.00 bill was changed into a coin, which we call the **"Loonie"** in 1987. It is a gold coloured coin with Queen Elizabeth on the face of the coin and the Common Loon on the back of the coin.

The $2.00 bill was changed into a coin, which we call the **"Toonie"**. It was first used on February 19, 1996. It is made of 2 metals, gold and silver coloured. The Queen is on the face of the coin and the Polar Bear is on the reverse side.

Canada decided to change its currency in 2010. In November 2011, the $100.00 and in March 2012, the $50.00 Bills were changed from paper to Polymer, which is a type of plastic. In April 2013, the $5.00, $10.00 and $20.00 bills completed the change.

Canadian bill currency
$5.00, $10.00, $20.00, $50.00, $100.00

This was done for a number of reasons:

1. It costs less to produce.
2. The bills last much longer.
3. They have newer security features and are more difficult to counterfeit.
4. They feature Braille Dots so that the seeing impaired have an easier time using their money.
5. Most importantly, they use a smaller eco-footprint, for future generations. Canada joined a growing list of countries which have moved in this direction.

Be careful - you can wash the Bills but do **Not** iron them!! I wonder why!

Comparison shopping in Toronto and at Home!

Item Purchased	Price in Toronto	Price at Home
Bag of Chips		
Newspaper		
Hot dog		
Subway or Bus Ticket		
Can of Coke		
Postcard		
Stamp for postcard		
Baseball Cap		
Souvenir (Your Choice)		
Bottle of water		
Your favourite candy		
Ice cream cone		

The R.O.M.

The Old & the New R.O.M.

Dinosaur Gallery

Specimen Collections

The R.O.M.

The Royal Ontario Museum is one of the world's leading museums of natural history and world cultures, home to over 6 million objects and 40 galleries of art, archaeology and natural science.

The ROM opened its doors on March 19, 1914 and instantly became an object of great pride. Throughout the century, several expansions added much needed space. The most remarkable visual addition - which opened June 2, 2007 - has been the Michael-Lee Chin Crystal, a special new symbol of Toronto for the 21st century. Mr. Chin gave $30 million to the ROM as a gift in thanks for the opportunities given to he and his family. He also hoped that this donation would inspire others to follow and become leaders.

The Crystal is made up of 5 interlocking self-supporting prism-like structures that are not attached to the original building, except for the bridge that joins them. Walk around the new and the old and see if this description is true. Make sure you also go outside to take a look.

Exhibits that must be seen include the dinosaur exhibit - with fossils from Alberta, gigantic fossil turtles and fish suspended from the ceiling, flying reptiles, North American totem poles near the main stairwell, Tyrannosaurus Rex with its 60 razor-sharp teeth, hands-on Biodiversity area on Level 2 and don't forget to visit the Bat Cave, also on level 3.

FUN FACT

The ROM is believed to be haunted by its first director, Dr. Charles Currelly.

Rumour has it that he walks around in his night-shirt in the East Asiatic section.

Keep your eyes open!!!

Have fun!! Watch out for bats and the ghost of Dr. Currelly.

The Royal Ontario Museum

Queen's Park - Ontario Legislature

Queen's Park - Ontario Legislature

Ontario's Coat of Arms
Above the North Door

Ontario Legislative buildings are home to the government of Ontario, the Lieutenant Governor of Ontario (Queen's representative) and offices for members of the provincial parliament (MPPs).

The present 5 story building - built in the Romanesque style - was officially opened April 4, 1893, by the acting Lieutenant Governor. As the population increased, it was necessary to expand the building. The North wing was added in 1909, the Whitney block in 1925, the MacDonald/Hepburn blocks in 1968 and the Mowat/Hearst blocks in 1969. The load bearing iron frame is covered in 10.5 million bricks made by the inmates of the Central Prison and Ontario's pink sandstone - giving it the name of the Pink Palace.

Don't forget to look up and around the building to see the various stone cravings, gargoyles, grotesques (odd/misshapen), and friezes (decorations). Above the North entrance, is a sandstone carving of Ontario's Coat of Arms, consisting of 3 maple leaves, the cross of St. George, black bear above the shield and the moose and deer on either side. The motto translation is "Loyal she began, loyal she remains."

This impressive structure sits in the middle of Queen's Park- one of the oldest city parks in Canada - near the University of Toronto. The south part of the park is home to statues of historic figures including Queen Victoria, King George V, John A. MacDonald (Canada's first Prime Minister) and John S. MacDonald (Ontario 1st Premier), no relation. There is also a war memorial - (west side), Ontario Police Memorial (east side), and Ontario Firefighters Memorial (south/east side). The Trillium Garden (south) is dedicated to the wildflower that is Ontario's official flower, a delicate white flower with 3 distinct leaves and pedals. Please do not pick them.

Free tours are available year round Monday to Friday between 9 am and 4:30 pm.

China Town

China Town

China Town

Chinatown is an ethnic community in the heart of downtown Toronto, extending along Dundas St. West and Spadina Avenue and is one of the largest in North America.

Toronto's Chinatown first appeared during the 1890's when American Chinese migrated from California and eastern United States because of racial tension and economic hard times. Hundreds of Chinese men helped build the Canadian Pacific Railway across Canada. Once this was completed, the men found housing close to the railway station because of convenience. Because other employment was hard to find, restaurants, grocery stores and hand laundries popped up and became successful Chinese businesses.

Present day Chinatown was formerly a Jewish district. If you've been to Kensington Market, you may have noticed the 2 active Synagogues remaining. During the 1960's, much of the Jewish population moved north and Chinese immigration and businesses expanded into this area.

Today the area is home to 2 major Chinese malls - Dragon City and Chinatown Centre. Street and store names are bilingual - Chinese and English. There are many restaurants for you to try some new and delicious Chinese food. Go to an all-you-can-eat buffet or try some dim sum - small, steamed portions. Pick up some herbs or other Chinese remedies. Check out some exotic fruit and vegetables that you may never have seen or tasted.

Chinatown is a unique community where visitors can see, smell, touch and taste all it has to offer!

Bi-lingual street signs

Chinese supermarket

My Favourite Things About Toronto

Art Gallery of Ontario - AGO

Henry Moore sculpture outside the AGO

The Art Gallery of Ontario is one of the largest and best known art museums in North America, with a collection of over 80,000 works of art from the 1st century to present day. Exhibits include the largest collection of Canadian art, work from the Renaissance and Baroque eras, European art, African art and a modern and contemporary collection.

The museum contains many sculptures, especially the Henry Moore Sculpture Centre. Did you see the sculpture outside at the south/east corner of the AGO? That is the work of Henry Moore. You'll find another Moore sculpture in front of Toronto's City Hall! You can't miss them.

The AGO sculpture will be moved in the near future to a new home in Grange Park, which is part of the Gallery. If you like, you may visit the Grange House and Park just behind the AGO.

The AGO dates back to 1910 when Goldwin Smith, a private citizen, gave his land and home to the gallery upon his death. Expansion throughout the century added various galleries which allowed local artists to display their works of art.

The AGO underwent a major facelift in 2004 by Toronto architect Frank Gehry. This was his first work in Canada! even though he was born in Toronto close to Kensington Market. 4 years later, the change was complete. AGO was increased by 47%, and included a new 4 story south wing covered in glass and blue titanium, a Gehry- designed spiral staircase in Walker court and a new glass and wood front - the Galleria Italia - spanning 180m (590 feet) along Dundas Street.

Now it is your turn to explore this amazing space.

Frank Gehry staircase in the AGO

Kensington Market

Kensington Market just off of China Town

Kensington Market covers a large multicultural neighbourhood in downtown Toronto. Its borders includes College St to the north, Dundas St. to the south, Bathurst St. to the west and Spadina Ave. to the east.

During the early 20th century, Kensington was populated by European Jews and some Italians. As a way to make money, imported items and gifts from the homelands of the many differing immigrant communities were sold and it became known as 'the Jewish market'. Jewish merchants

operated small shops: tailors, furriers and bakers. Over 30 synagogues were established for the 60,000 worshippers. Today, 2 synagogues remain - Anshei Minsk on St. Andrew Street and Kiever Synagogue on Bellevue Avenue.

After World War II, the Jewish population moved north and large numbers of immigrants from the Azores (Portugal) arrived. As the years went by, new groups of people from the Caribbean and East Asia continued to change the community.

Today, Kensington Market continues to be a multicultural community and a national historic site. You will find a plaque in Bellevue Square given to Kensington Market in 2006.

The market is filled with a mix of food, stores selling a variety of meats, fish, produce, bakeries, spices, dry goods, cheese, new and vintage clothing, discount and surplus stores. Stop by and explore the gift shops for local and global gifts, vintage clothing shops and unique kitchen gadgets stores. Check out a few of the alternative bookstores in Kensington.

On Saturdays and some afternoons, you are able to walk freely down the middle of the streets. During the summer, several Sundays are car-free days. Live music, dancing, street theatre and various games are some of the special events you will have the chance to experience. Enjoy!

The Jewish Community settled in the area in the early 1920's

Which is the Correct Spelling?

1.	stret car	street car
2.	Spadina Ave.	Spidina Ave.
3.	High Park	Hyde Park
4.	Scince Centre	Science Centre
5.	sculpture	sculture
6.	Harbourfront	Harborfront
7.	Eyelids	Islands
8.	City Hall	Citee Hal
9.	hockey	Hookeey
10.	St. Mikell's Cathedrill	St. Michael's Cathedral
11.	Fort Yourke	Fort York
12.	soldiers	solders
13.	St. Lawence Markit	St. Lawrence Market
14.	Fairy Boat	Ferry Boat
15.	Red Rocket	Read Roket

True or False

1. The C.N. Tower is not in Toronto. T or F
2. Ripley's Aquarium is next to the C.N. Tower. T or F
3. There is a Military Fort in the centre of Toronto. T or F
4. You can walk to Centre Island. T or F
5. You can skate in August at City Hall. T or F
6. There are four Gargoyles on Old City Hall Tower. T or F
7. Osgoode gate was used to keep out farm animals. T or F
8. Canada's money is made of paper. T or F
9. You can collect pennies in Canada. T or F
10. They say there is a ghost in the R.O.M. T or F
11. The Legislature is in Queen's Park. T or F
12. There is a Synagogue in Kensington Market. T or F
13. William Lyon Mackenzie was the 3rd Mayor of Toronto. T or F
14. The Hockey Hall of Fame is not in Toronto. T or F
15. You can buy sports equipment at St. Lawrence Market. T or F

St. Michael's Cathedral

St. Michael's Cathedral

St. Michael's Cathedral

St. Michael's Cathedral - home to the Roman Catholic Archdiocese of Toronto - is one of the oldest churches in the city.

Father Power, chosen as the first bishop in 1841, selected Toronto as the new western diocese of the Roman Catholic Church. St. Paul's - built in 1822 - was the first Catholic parish church in the city. As Toronto and its population increased, Bishop Power felt that a new church building was needed for the rapidly growing Catholic population. By 1845, he bought the land at a cost of £1800 ($3650. Canadian/$2600. US) of which $500. came from his own funds. Construction began on April 7,1845. The church was blessed September 1848 but the building remained empty. There was no more money. Toronto's second bishop - Bishop de Charbonnel - finding the cathedral empty, undecorated and in debt, appealed to the parishioners for funds. Using his own personal monies (family was wealthy), de Charbonnel had stained glass windows designed and the Stations of the Cross imported from France. He also added the chapels in the north and south sides as well as to the left and right of the sanctuary.

St. Michael's Cathedral is located at 200 Church St. but its main entrance is on its west side off Bond St. The architectural style is similar to a 13th or 14th century simplified Gothic revival cathedral. The high altar is in the east end of the building, facing Jerusalem. At its tallest point, the tower reaches 79m. (260 feet). A tall iron fence surrounds the perimeter. The magnificent 'Crucifixion of Jesus' stained glass was hand blown and imported from France in 1858.

Since 2011, major renovations have occurred. Beneath the floor of the cathedral, lies a crypt where several of Toronto's bishops were buried - from Bishop Michael Power to a worker killed during its construction. This will be dug out, reinforced and become part of a new crypt chapel. At the rear of the church, a beautiful stained glass window known as the 'Great West Window', was invisible from the inside, hidden behind the massive pipes of the church's original organ (1880). With a new organ (2016), the pipes will stand on either side of the window allowing natural light to filter inside. A new 260-seat balcony will also be added.

The ceiling is being repainted by hand with 22/23 karat gold-leaf illustrating twinkling stars, forcing visitors to look up! New bronze doors will welcome parishioners and visitors.

Inside St. Michael's Cathedral

St. James Cathedral

St. James Anglican Cathedral

Inside St. James Cathedral

St. James Cathedral is home to the oldest congregation of Toronto and is the Seat of the Anglican Church of Canada. Its tower is the highest in Canada (93m./305feet) and holds 12 bells that chime a unique ring throughout the downtown area.

The first Anglican service was held on this site in 1793 and a wooden church was built in 1807 with the help of the soldiers from Fort York. During the War of 1812, it was used as a hospital and later damaged and robbed by American soldiers. In 1832, a large stone church was built but burned down in 1839. The first Anglican bishop of Toronto - Reverend John Strachan- built a cathedral in its place but it was completely destroyed by fire for the second time in 1849.

Without enough money to rebuild, Toronto's first architectural competition was open with hopes of getting a "new church in the Gothic style". With success, Bishop Strachan lay the cornerstone in 1850 and the first service was held June 19, 1853.

Inside the cathedral is a special covered pew for the Governor General at the front of the nave. The stained glass windows were made by Tiffany and Company of New York and dedicated to William Jarvis - who was an Upper Canada official. The original organ (1863/1889) was rebuilt twice and has 5,001 pipes. Distinguished visitors have included members of the Royal Family - Queen Elizabeth II and Prince Philip in 1997, Prince Charles and Princess Diana with their sons William and Harry in 1991 as well as Archbishop Desmond Tutu in 2004.

To the east of the Cathedral is St. James Park, an urban space with walkways, park benches and a large ornamental gazebo in the middle. Formal gardens are located to the south.

Mackenzie House

Mackenzie House

Mackenzie House is a historic museum and the last house of Toronto's first Mayor and leader of the Rebellion of 1837, William Lyon Mackenzie. This house was given to him as a gift upon his retirement from friends and supporters for his years of community service.

Mackenzie was born (1795) and raised in Scotland, emigrating to Upper Canada (Ontario) in 1820. In 1824, he published his first issue of the Colonial Advocate and became a strong voice of the new Reform movement - preferring responsible government and opposing British rule. When the Reformers won a majority in 1834 in the newly created Toronto City Council, Mackenzie was elected its first mayor. He was defeated 2 years later in 1836. In the fall of 1837, he turned his focus to an armed revolt, calling for American-style democracy. This revolt was poorly organized, lacked leadership and discipline. The Loyalists quickly defeated Mackenzie's rebels, forcing him to flee to New York State where he spent 10 years writing. After a government pardon, he returned to Canada, resuming his writing and political career. Upon retirement in 1857, he moved to the Bond St. home where he died.

Mackenzie House is a fully-functional 19th century home and printshop built in the Georgian style, similar to the one used by Mackenzie to publish newspapers. The gallery wing- built in 1967- displays changing exhibits. The house, courtyard garden, printing press and costumed staff show what life was like in the 19th century. Mackenzie House is said to be the most haunted house in Toronto - possibly Canada. Although Mackenzie only lived here for 2 years - passing away in his bedroom on the second floor- there are reports of eerie reminders of both Mackenzie, his wife and some of his children. The ghost of a bald man in a wig and frock has often been seen around, especially in the area of the 3rd floor bedroom. Cold spots and activities such as footsteps and the basement printing press starting up have been reported by staff and visitors.

Maybe you'll have a chance of experiencing something unique and unusual!!

Hockey Hall of Fame, in the former Bank of Montreal built in 1886

"Our Game" Bronze Sculpture by Edie Parker

Hockey Hall of Fame

Hockey is the sport that defines Canadians of all ages. The Hockey Hall of Fame - located at the bottom of Yonge and Front Street - offers something for everyone. Spread over 7,000 sq. m.(65,000 sq. feet), you will be able to see the best collection of hockey artifacts from all over the world. You will be able to challenge your shooting and goalkeeping skills. You will see exhibits dedicated to hockey's greatest players, teams and their achievements. Larger-than-life statues, a replica of a NHL dressing room, and the Stanley Cup are exhibits you can touch and explore. Don't forget to look at the portraits and biographies of each of the 388 honoured members of the HHOF. Make sure you see the newest "Stanley's Game Seven" - a 3D film combining live action, computer generated 3D animation and classic footage from the best moments in hockey.

The Hockey Hall of Fame is located in an extravagant, ornate building - a former Bank of Montreal - that is older than the Stanley Cup. Completed in 1886, many parts of this building have been kept such as the large stain-glass dome and Greek-style pediments (triangle gables) and dentils (rectangle blocks) around the outside.

FUN FACT

Touching the Stanley Cup is every player's goal. You can only touch the cup if you've earned it. It is an unwritten rule that you can't touch the cup until you've won it.

What do you think?

True??   False??

St. Lawrence Market

St. Lawrence Market

Inside St. Lawrence Market

St. Lawrence Market - located at Front Street East and Jarvis Street - is a major public market and is named the best food market in the world by National Geographic. The market consists of 3 buildings - St. Lawrence South, St. Lawrence North and St. Lawrence Hall.

This market originated in 1893 when people were able to get together to buy and sell their cattle, sheep, poultry, goods and other provisions - but only on Saturdays. By 1820, a wooden structure was built. This became a Centre for the city's social life where auctions took place, public punishments were carried out and people wandered the market. In 1831, this structure was replaced by a brick building with arched entrances. Toronto's Great Fire of 1849 destroyed its northern side. On this site, St. Lawrence Hall was built along with a new market. Replacement of the north market occurred in 1904 and 1968. The south market was built in 1845 and became Toronto's City Hall. It was rebuilt in 1850 and 1904 and renovated in 1972. Toronto is now in the process of replacing the North building with a new 4-storey structure with an atrium.

St. Lawrence South has 2 main floors. The upper floor has over 50 vendors selling fruit, meat, cheese, vegetables, sandwiches, arts and crafts and kitchen supplies. At the north end of the building, you can see remnants of the old city hall. The Market Gallery displays different exhibitions explaining Toronto's history, art, culture and programs for school and community groups. Visitors can always join in.

The Farmers' Market is open on Saturdays from 5 AM to 3 PM. The south market is open from 8 AM to 6 PM - 7 PM on Friday - closed Sunday and Monday. The Antique Market is open Sunday from 5AM to 5PM.

Enjoy the sights and sounds and bring your appetites!!

Distillery District

Smoke stack - Distillery District 1832

Distillery Historic District

The Distillery District - located southeast of Front St. East and Parliament St - is a 13 acre district made up of more than 40 heritage buildings and 10 streets. It is the largest collection of Victorian-era industrial architecture in North America.

Gooderham and Worts Distillery (original name) was founded in 1832. By the 1860's, it was the largest distillery in the world, delivering over 7.6 million litres (2 million gallons) of whiskey. Being close to both railways and water, made transport easier. By the late 20th century, distillery operations decreased and the area was left vacant. The 1990's brought redevelopment and investment, allowing the buildings to be preserved and protected.

Today, this historic brick-paved area has become a National Historic Site (1988). Its 40 buildings are home to boutiques, art galleries, antiques, restaurants, cafes, coffee houses and a microbrewery, the Mill Street Brewery. It is also home to the Soul-Pepper Theatre Company and various drama productions by the students from George Brown College.

Car traffic is restricted to the outside perimeter of the district, allowing pedestrians to walk and enjoy the sights. Check out the large sculptures installed along the lanes and the 31m.(100 feet) chimney stack that sits on top of the Boiler House complex. Other main structures not to miss include the Stone House Distillery, the Boiler House (landmark), the Tank House (landmark), the Stables, the Cannery, various tank houses, the Crapper, the outhouse and the Pump house (landmark).

If you're visiting during the summer, a Sunday market gives visitors the opportunities to taste treats such as empanadas and organic maple syrup. If you're coming in the winter, the Christmas Market ('mid November to just before Christmas) is an event not to miss.

Toronto's Haunted Places

Halls of U. of T.

Toronto has over 200 years worth of haunted happenings that are worthwhile exploring. Whether or not you believe in this, the stories are fun to hear.

The University of Toronto is home to many spirits wandering the grounds of its campus. Here are a few to look out for.

A Russian stonemason was murdered by a fellow mason who was teasing him during the building of the college in 1850. The body was buried under a stairwell. Look for the axe mark on the door next to **Croft Chapter House** and 2 spooky gargoyles outside the house.

Soldier's Tower U. of T.

Soldiers Tower - connects Hart House with University College. A repairman fell to his death in the 1930's. Students say that his spirit walks near the tower and strange lights shine through the windows at night.

Massey College - One of Canada's famous novelist Robertson Davis told the college Master that he'd return from the beyond. Davis died in 1995. Students claim to hear odd noises coming from empty rooms. Is it Davis??

Royal Conservatory of Music - Music students claim to see the spirit of a lady in red, usually in the halls of the second or third floors.

Ontario Legislature

Ontario's Legislative Buildings - Queens Park - have at least 4 spooks wandering around. In the mid 19th century, this area belonged to an insane asylum (hospital). The 4 ghosts include a "white lady", another woman who covers her face with an apron, an angry-looking soldier and a "hanging lady" dangling from a hook in an underground tunnel.

Fort York

Fort York - Witnesses have reported seeing phantom (ghost)!soldiers, dressed in the original red coats, in the grounds after dark.

Massey Hall has sightings of a man dressed in old clothes who wanders around the backstage area as well as an elderly couple who have been spotted in the aisles late at night.

Old City Hall - Judges have heard mysterious footsteps and have felt their robes tugged when they are near the rear staircase. The last 2 men to hang in Canada (1962) are said to occupy courtroom 125 where they were sentenced.

Osgoode Hall is home to a ghostly woman seen walking the halls as well as voices of people in empty chambers.

10 Interesting Facts About Toronto

Red Rocket

1. Toronto's streetcar system - the "Red Rocket" - is the largest system in the Western world.
2. More passengers (65 million) go through Union Station than Pearson International Airport (41 million), yearly.

Toronto Maple Leafs

3. The Toronto Maple Leafs have not won a Stanley Cup since 1967 but have such loyal fans that tickets for the games are always sold out.

4. Toronto is home to one of the world's best film festival - TIFF - Toronto International Film Festival - every year in September.

5. Babe Ruth hit his first professional home run at Centre Island.

The beginning of Yonge Street

6. Toronto's longest street is Yonge Street, beginning at the foot of Yonge and Queen Quay. It's 1,896 km. (1,138 miles) long and ends at the Ontario/Manitoba border at Rainy River. Once you pass Barrie, it is called Highway 11.

7. TV show "Suits" is filmed the corner of Bay and Adelaide St. Other shows that are filmed in Toronto include Flashpoint, Cash Cab, Orphan Black, Rookie Blue and Saving Hope.

8. Famous Torontonians include Drake, The Weeknd, Jim Carrey, Christopher Plummer, Megan Follows, Shawn Mendes, John Candy, Michael Cera, Mike Myers and K'naan, who wrote and sang "Waving Flag" for World Cup 2010.

Caribana in Toronto

9. Toronto is host to Caribana- a sharing of Caribbean culture. It is the largest single day parade in North America, about 3.6 km (2 miles) long with over 10,000 costumed participants.

C.N. Tower

10. On a clear day, you can see the north shore of New York State from the CN Tower.

Aga Khan Museum

The Aga Khan Museum

One of the many artifacts - Aga Khan Museum

The Aga Khan Museum is North America's first museum dedicated to presenting an overview of the artistic, intellectual and scientific contributions of 11 centuries of Muslim civilizations. The 10,000 square metre structure is set within formal gardens and surrounded by a large park - Aga Khan Park.

His Highness, the Aga Khan, who is the spiritual leader to 15 million Ismali Muslims around the world, took the first step to create a museum that would show all aspects of the people of Islam, their history and culture as well as their ethnic language, religious and social differences.

Toronto was chosen by the Aga Khan because of its multicultural community. He acknowledged Canada's direction in building a diverse society.

Artifacts include ceramics, metal work, ivory, stone, textiles, glass/rock/crystal objects and paintings covering all periods of Islamic history. Manuscripts include the earliest known copy of "The Canon of Medicine" dated back to 1052. Over 1,000 objects include excellent examples of Quran manuscripts that show the variety of script, media and decorative styles.

Reflecting fountains Aga Khan Museum

Science Centre

Fun with Science

Ontario Science Centre

Ontario Science Centre is located about 11 km.(6.6 miles) northeast of downtown Toronto. It consists of 3 main buildings connected by a series of bridges and escalators and follows the natural flow of the Don River Ravine. Unlike a traditional museum, many of the exhibits are interactive and others host live demonstrations.

The centre has several hundred exhibits including geology, the science of nature, the science of astronomy, how to play music, technology, human anatomy and communication.

The state-of-the-art Planetarium within the centre includes meteorites from Mars, cosmic rays, black holes and a space chair that is really a rocket.

See stories of athletes, survivalists, extreme sport enthusiasts and others who broke through barriers and boundaries in the Astra Zeneca Human Edge.

In the Living Earth, touch a tornado, hang out in a cave, get close to cockroaches and poison dart frogs. Do you think your parents will be joining you? Word Harp, Ferrofluid Fountains and Pipe Dreams feature fun, hands-on exhibits.

Do not forget to see what's playing at the Omnimax theatre, a screen 4,500 times bigger than an average TV screen with sound from 44 speakers.

Toronto Zoo

Welcome to Toronto Zoo

The Toronto Zoo, located near the Rouge River, is the largest zoo in Canada. It is divided into 7 zoo-geographic regions - Indo-Malaya, Africa, Americas, Tundra Trek, Australia, Eurasia and Canadian Domain. Many of the 5,000 + animals, representing over 450 species, live in either tropical pavilions or outdoor pavilions - whatever is their natural environment.

The Indo-Malaya area has 4 outdoor exhibits that display Indian rhino, Sumatran orang-utan, Mandarin ducks and rare Sumatran tigers.

The African Savanna features olive baboons, white rhinos, spotted hyenas and Masai giraffe. It is home to the world's largest indoor gorilla exhibit. You will also get a chance to see 3 white African Lions who have made Toronto their home since 2012.

In the Canadian Domain you will see elk, bison, moose, bald eagle, cougar, Lynx and grizzly bears.

Polar bear cub playing in the snow

The Americas include animals from both North and South America. Some of the most popular ones are two-toed sloths, American alligators, beavers, river otters and giant Pacific octopus. The Mayan Temple Ruins are home to jaguars, macaws, spider monkeys and flamingoes.

The Australian Pavilion has grey kangaroo, wallabies, emus, wombats, kookaburras, cockatoos and Komodo dragons - a gift from the President of Indonesia.

Eurasia is the oldest and quietest area of the zoo. Its inhabitants include snow leopards, red pandas, horses, camels, Barbary apes and yak. As of May 2013, this area is now home to 2 giant pandas. October 13, 2015 saw the birth of 2 red panda cubs. They were introduced to the public in mid-March 2016 when they were 5 months old.

The Tundra Trek is one of the newest exhibits and includes Arctic animals such as reindeer, snowy owls, snow geese, Arctic foxes, wolves and Canada's polar bears, along with, the new addition Juno, who was born on November 11, 2014. She is the official "live" mascot of the Canadian Army.

While exploring the zoo, make sure you visit the Discovery Zone - an area featuring changing themes and exhibits. A must see is the water park Splash Island and Waterside Theatre where you'll see live demonstrations. The Kids Zoo enables you to interact with various animals.

Black Creek Pioneer Village

Wagon Ride at Pioneer Village

Festival at Pioneer Village

Black Creek Pioneer Village

Black Creek Pioneer Village is an open-air heritage museum, located west of York University and overlooking Black Creek, a branch of the Humber River. The Village gives visitors a chance to know what it was like to have lived in rural Ontario in the early-to-mid 19th century.

Pioneer Village consists of over forty 19th century buildings, decorated according to early 1860's style with period furniture. Noteworthy buildings include Dalziel barn - the oldest Pennsylvania barn in Canada, period houses, the original Stong family farm buildings, a water-powered grist mill (grinding grain), a general store, a blacksmith shop, a hotel, a church and a one-room schoolhouse.

Visitors have opportunities to participate in various hands-on activities such as open-fire cooking, bread-making, weaving, milling, black smithing, sewing, printing and more. You can also question the knowledgeable and friendly staff who are dressed in period costumes.

Enjoy your day by taking a step back in time!

High Park

Colborne Lodge High Park

Grenadier Pond High Park

High Park

High Park is Toronto's largest public park, covering 400 acres of land in the heart of the city, stretching from Bloor St. (North) to just north of Lake Ontario (south).

John Howard - an architect and engineer for the City of Toronto - purchased 160 acres of land in 1836 to be used as a sheep farm. Here he built and designed a cottage - Colborne Lodge - in 1837 for himself and his wife, Jemima Meikle. They named this land "High Park" because it was located on the highest point of land from the lake.

In 1873, Howard and his wife agreed to give this property to the City of Toronto but there were a few restrictions. The most important ones were that the park was to be always called High Park, the citizens of Toronto were to have free use and enjoyment of the park, the Howards would continue to live in their home until their death and no alcohol ever was to be served in the park. All the conditions still stand today. The Howards are buried across the street from their home, Colborne Lodge. Look for a stone monument that has an ornate (fancy) fencing.

The landscape of High Park is hilly and slopes southward. Two deep ravines extend the full north-south length of the park. The Eastern part of the park will give you access to a spring-fed pond, grassy area for picnics, an adventure playground and the zoo, home to American Bison, emu, llamas, peacocks, deer, wallaby, yaks and sheep. It is located along Deer Pen Road.

The central section - perfect for picnics and sports - is a large plain, mostly along the northern boundary and narrow to a point that overlooks Lake Ontario. Here you will find Colborne Lodge, now a museum showing the furnishings and art work of the Howards. Black oak Savannah trees populate this area.

Grenadier Pond is located on the western edge of the park, extending southward. Two stories are part of this pond. One is that the British Grenadier soldiers fell through the thin ice when crossing the pond as they tried to defend the city in the War of 1812. Their bodies were never discovered. Another belief is that the pond is bottomless- it's depth cannot be measured due to the amount of mud. Nevertheless, fishing, ice skating and boating are regular pastimes. An ornamental garden area extends from the hill to the east of Grenadier Pond up to Colborne Lodge. You will find a rock garden near Grenadier Cafe. North of the lodge is High Park's Children Garden.

Don't forget to visit Grenadier Cafe for a bite to eat, visit the organic market on weekends, ride the High Park Trackless Train that circles the park only in the summer and take a dip in High Park Pool.

As you can see, there is much to do and see in High Park. Enjoy the Howards gift to the city.

Places Not To Miss!

Bata Shoe Museum

Philosopher's Walk U. of T.

Casa Loma

Places Not To Miss

Bata Shoe Museum

- St. George and Bloor
- world's largest footwear museum with over 13,600 items from around the world and throughout history to present time
- see Shaquille O'Neal size 22 athletic shoe

Roy Thompson Hall

- 60 Simcoe St. and King St.
- concert hall seating 2,630
- home to the Toronto Symphony Orchestra and Toronto Mendelssohn Choir

Bell Lightbox

- King and John St.
- headquarters for TIFF - Toronto International Film Festival
- home to 5 screen cinemas, film library, changing exhibits, galleries and eateries

Eaton Centre

- Yonge and Dundas St.
- top tourist attraction with over 175 stores
- includes Toronto's PATH - an underground pedestrian walkway from Eaton Centre (north) to Queens Quay (south)

Canada's Wonderland

- north of Toronto
- Canada's first and largest theme park
- over 200 attractions, 68 thrilling rides, splash works, water park and live shows

Philosophers Walk/University of Toronto

- a scenic footpath running north / south, west of the R.O.M.
- surrounded by several landmarks including the Royal Conservatory of Music, Trinity College, U of T Faculty of Law

Gardiner Museum

- 111 Queens Park - across from the R.O.M.
- Canada's natural ceramic museum
- over 2,900 pieces from Ancient Americas, Italian Renaissance, English Delftware, Chinese/Japanese/European porcelain

Casa Loma

- a Gothic revival castle built on a hill by Sir Henry Pellatt - one of Canada's top financier
- largest private home in Canada from 1914 to 1923, with electricity
- included first electric elevator, central vacuum system, 52 telephones, and the first flushing toilet.
- underground tunnel connects to hunting lodge and stables

Coming Home

1. How are you getting to the airport or train station? ____________
2. What city are you leaving from? ______________________
3. What is the name of the airport or train station? ____________
4. What time did you arrive at the airport or train station? ________

5. What airline or rail line are you travelling with? ______________

6. What is your flight number or train number? ______________

7. What is your seat number? ______________

8. Did you depart on time? ______________

9. What did you eat on your return trip? ______________

____

10. What did you do on your return trip home? ______________

____

____

11. Where did you land or disembark by train? ______________

12. Did you go through Customs? ______________

13. Did they stamp your passport? ______________

14. How did you get home? ______________

15. What time did you enter your home? ______________

16. Will you be happy to sleep in your own bed tonight? ______________

17. What was the best thing about your vacation with your family?

____

____

18. Would you return to Toronto? ______________

19. Why or why not? ______________

____

____

20. Would your parents return to Toronto? ______________

Hope you had a great time!
Barbara and Therese

Things You Don't Want To Forget!

Photo credits

Photo #	Page #	Description	Photographer/Dreamtime
Book Cover		CN Tower through doors of U. of T.	Wes Adams - U of T
3	5	airplane	Rawpixelimages
5	10	Map of Canada	Indos82
6	12	Canada with prof. flags	Michael Baranski
8	14	Ontario Flag	Lester69
10	16	Ontario Map	Rainer Lesniewski
12	20	View through glass floor	Richard Billingham
20	28	Ferry boat	Andres Garcia Martin
42	52	St. Michael's Cathedral	Thevirex
43	52	St. Michael's inside	rmnoa357 - Shutterstock
45	54	St. James Inside	Yelena Rodriquez
63	66	Caribana	Lucy Cherniak
67	70	Ontario Science Centre	Ontario Science Centre
68	70	Cryo Demonstration at the Science Centre	Ontario Science Centre
69	72	Welcome to Toronto Zoo	Mira Agron
70	72	Polar Bear in snow	Andy White
71	74	Wagon ride Pioneer Village	Lucy Cherniak
72	74	Girls Festival Pioneer Vill.	Lucy Cherniak
77	78	Casa Loma	Saphire Ovadia
Back Cover		Toronto Poster	Ladoga - Shutterstock

Thank you to the following people who donated their images to this book:

Olivia Mirski
Ramon
Chloe Hollands

Contact the Authors

Email

goingtotravelguides@gmail.com

Website

goingtotravelguides.com

Facebook:

Going to - Travel Guide and Journal for Kids

CPSIA information can be obtained
at www.ICGtesting.com
Printed in the USA
LVOW01s2054021116
510793LV00007B/14/P

9 781773 020877